Since 1888, *National Geographic* magazine has provided its readers a wealth of information and helped us understand the world in which we live. Insightful articles, supported by gorgeous photography and impeccable research, bring the mission of the National Geographic Society front and center: to inspire people to care about the planet. The *Explore* series delivers *National Geographic* to you in the same spirit. Each of the books in this series presents the best articles on popular and relevant topics in an accessible format. In addition, each book highlights the work of National Geographic Explorers, photographers, and writers. Explore the world of *National Geographic*. You will be inspired.

ON THE COVER
A river in the Skardu Valley, nestled in the Karakoram mountain range in Pakistan

THE HIMALAYA

LETTER FROM THE EDITORS

About 40 million years ago, two of the massive tectonic plates that make up Earth's crust began to slowly collide, one moving from the Northern Hemisphere and the other moving from the Southern Hemisphere. As these two plates shoved together, the Himalayan Mountains began to rise. The collision produced Mount Everest—at 29,035 feet the world's highest mountain—and more than 110 other peaks that top 24,000 feet. Satellite images of the range today show great expanses of gleaming white peaks, ribbons of ice, sharp shadows of summits and ridges, brown valleys, and high plateaus. It is hard to imagine anyone living in that rugged landscape. Yet the mountains, covering all or part of 12 countries, are home to people, cultures, animals, and stories you will be glad to know.

It's tempting to think that the rugged nature of the land is responsible for the kinds of people who are born in the Himalaya and those who are drawn to visit there. In this book you'll find articles adapted from *National Geographic* about several of these intriguing people. You'll meet climbers, adventurers, anthropologists, archaeologists, and an athletic photographer. These explorers come for the sport or to explore the region's fascinating history.

You'll also learn about the Sherpas of Nepal who guide visitors to the mountains and conservationists in several countries who track and defend the hard-to-find snow leopard. You'll meet Edmund Hillary and Tenzing Norgay, the first to summit Everest, and climbers who have dared the peak of K2, a soaring Himalayan mountain that is considered even harder to climb than Everest. Before you put down this book, you may be planning a visit to one of the inspiring locations you've read about.

If you're not sure you really want to go, think about Hillary's answer to the question of whether an ice ridge near Everest's peak would hold his weight. He wrote: "There was only one way to find out."

Baby snow leopards begin hunting at three months of age. They remain under their mothers' protection through their first winter.

The Modest Hero of
Everest

BY PETER MILLER AND MICHAEL KLESIUS

Adapted from "50 Years: The Hero,"
by Peter Miller and "50 Years:
The History," by Michael Klesius,
in *National Geographic*, May 2003

HERO OF THE MOUNTAIN
Though Edmund Hillary was prepared
to climb Mount Everest, the attention
that followed surprised him.

What does it take to stand on top of the world?

In 2003, *National Geographic* ran a series of articles to commemorate the 50th anniversary of the first ascent of Mount Everest. Sir Edmund Hillary was featured in several of the stories.

First at the Top

New Zealander Edmund Hillary and Tenzing Norgay from Nepal were the first ever to stand on top of the world's highest mountain. They were part of a 1953 British expedition under the leadership of John Hunt. "Everyone [on the team] rightly believed," Hunt wrote, "that he [Hillary] had a vital part to play in getting at least two members of the team on top."

The British first speculated in 1852 that Mount Everest was the highest in the world. In the following century, several expeditions—aided by **Sherpas**—attempted to reach the summit. Until 1953, none succeeded.

In the 50 years following Hillary and Norgay's triumph, more than 1,200 men and women from 63 nations have reached the summit of Mount Everest. In the same period, 175 climbers have died in the attempt. Anyone aiming for the summit must face the Death Zone, the region of thin air above 26,000 feet. Survival there is never certain. "There are a hundred ways to get killed on Everest," says Pete Athans, who has reached the summit seven times.

STAYING IN TOUCH
The 1953 Everest expedition used this radio set for communications.

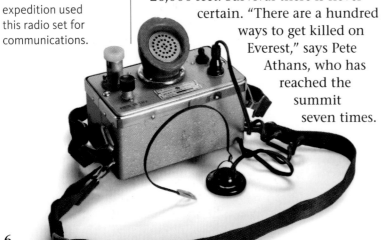

Humble Man, Bold Climber

Edmund Hillary was a modest hero. Shortly after the climb, he received word that Queen Elizabeth planned to make him a knight: Sir Edmund. He was taken aback. "I didn't feel I was the ideal sort of person who should have a title," he said. For one thing, he couldn't see strolling around his hometown in New Zealand in his old work clothes, as a knight! He remembers saying to himself, "I'll have to buy a new pair of overalls."

Hillary was a tall beekeeper from the fringes of the British Empire. He had learned to climb in New Zealand's Southern Alps in the winter (the off-season for bees). He was as bold on ice and snow as anyone on the Everest climbing team.

In the years that followed his conquest of Everest, Hillary pursued a number of new goals. He led expeditions on first ascents of several Himalayan peaks. He went to the South Pole in support of a British scientific party crossing Antarctica. He wrote books about his adventures. Having given up beekeeping, he signed on as a camping consultant to the Sears department store chain in 1963. He tested new tent designs on vacations with his wife, Louise, and their three children.

Catastrophe struck in 1975, when a small plane carrying Louise and their youngest child crashed near Kathmandu, the capital of Nepal high in the Himalaya. The two were on their way to join Sir Edmund. He and his brother Rex were building a hospital with local Sherpas and volunteers in a Nepali village. It took many years for Sir Edmund to recover from the loss. He took some comfort in the physical labor of his aid projects in the Everest region, and eventually he remarried.

"My Story" by Sir Edmund Hillary

Fifty years after his historic ascent of Mount Everest, Hillary provided his admirers with a valuable narrative. In "My Story" he gives a vivid account of reaching the summit along with the Sherpa and fellow climber Tenzing Norgay. He also describes his years of service and friendship with the Nepali people.

Ever since the morning of May 29, 1953, when Tenzing Norgay and I became the first climbers to step onto the summit of Mount Everest, I've been called a great adventurer. The truth is, I'm just a rough old New Zealander who has enjoyed many challenges in his life. In fact, as I look back after 50 years, getting to the top of Everest seems less important, in many ways, than other steps I've taken along the way—steps to improve the lives of my Sherpa friends in Nepal and to protect the culture and beauty of the Himalaya.

Not that I wasn't excited to reach the top of the world. I remember when Tenzing and I faced the icy, narrow final ridge to the summit. Some

on our team had predicted the ridge would be impossible to climb. . . . After attaching fresh oxygen bottles to our masks, we set off. I led the way, hacking a line of steps with my ice ax. After about an hour we came to a 40-foot-high rock **buttress** barring our path—quite a problem at nearly 29,000 feet. An ice **cornice** was overhanging the rock on the right with a long crack inside it. Beneath the cornice the mountain fell away at least 10,000 feet to the Kangshung Glacier. Would the cornice hold if I tried to go up? There was only one way to find out.

Jamming my **crampons** into the ice behind me, I somehow wriggled my way to the top of the crack, using every handhold I could find. For the first time I felt confident that we were going to make it all the way. To the right I saw a rounded snow dome and kept cutting steps upward. In less than an hour I reached the crest of the ridge, with nothing but space in every direction. Tenzing joined me, and to our great delight and relief we stood on top of Mount Everest.

In the years that followed our climb, I returned many times to the Everest region with my mountaineering friends and built up a close relationship with the Sherpas, spending a great deal of time in their homes and with their families. I admired their courage and strength, but I quickly realized that there were many things they lacked in their society that we just took for granted back in New Zealand such as schools or medical facilities. . . .

So over the years I've done lots of expeditions and projects in remote parts of the world—some big ones and many small ones. I've stood at both the North and South Poles as well as on the world's highest peak. When I look back over my life, though, I have little doubt that the most worthwhile things I have done have not been getting to the summits of great mountains or to the extremes of the Earth. My most important projects have been the building and maintaining of schools and medical clinics for my dear friends in the Himalaya and helping restore their beautiful monasteries too.

I clearly remember the happy day when we first opened the Khumjung school with only 47 children in scruffy Sherpa clothes—but with rosy cheeks and beaming smiles. Now one of them is a pilot of a Boeing 767 and others are important executives in travel, business, and nonprofit organizations.

These are the memories I will carry with me always.

LIKE FATHER, LIKE SON
Peter Hillary, son of Sir Edmund, greets well-wishers in Katmandu, Nepal, on his return from Mount Everest on May 28, 2002.

Closing the Loop

On May 25, 2002, Sir Edmund got a telephone call. It was from his son. "Dad, it's Peter. We're on the summit." The 47-year-old was part of a National Geographic expedition to Everest. They were commemorating the 50th anniversary of his father's climb. With him were other sons—Jamling Norgay, Tenzing's son, and Brent Bishop, Barry Bishop's son. Barry Bishop had been part of the first American team to reach the summit of Mount Everest, in 1963.

"Well, take it easy on the way down," Sir Edmund cautioned.

Editor's note: Sir Edmund Hillary died in January 2008. He had lived to celebrate the 50th anniversary of his historic climb and receive the gratitude of the many Nepali people he had helped through his tireless efforts.

THINK ABOUT IT! |||||||||||||||||||||||||||||||

1 **Evaluate** What do you think was Hillary's greater contribution to the world, his climbing or his work with the Nepali people?

2 **Describe Geographic Information** What do you learn in the article about why Mount Everest is very difficult to climb?

3 **Find Main Ideas and Details** What is the main impression that the article gives of the character of Edmund Hillary, and what details support that impression?

BACKGROUND & VOCABULARY

buttress *n.* (BUH-trihs) in architecture, a broad, heavy structure built to support a wall or other standing structure; here, an obstruction

cornice *n.* (KOR-nuhs) in mountain climbing, an overhanging ledge of snow or ice projecting from the side of a ridge or peak

crampons *n.* (KRAM-pahnz) the spikes attached to shoes to make it easier to grip the surface

Sherpa *n.* (SHUR-puh) the members of an ethnic group in northern Nepal, many of whom have found work as guides for mountaineers; Tenzing Norgay was a Sherpa.

The SHERPAS

BY T. R. REID

Adapted from "The Sherpas," by T. R. Reid,
in *National Geographic*, May 2003

A LONG, ICY TRIP
A group of Sherpas guide yaks
carrying supplies to Mount Everest
base camp, the starting point for
climbers aiming for the summit.

MARKET DAY
Shoppers often walk for days to stock up at Namche Bazaar's Saturday market. They return home with everything from goats to solar panels.

Tough, friendly, and skilled in business, the Sherpas of Nepal's Khumbu region have gotten rich from high-altitude tourism. They guide **trekkers** through their homeland step by challenging step. Writer T. R. Reid spoke with several Sherpas about their lives.

Big Business in Nepal

Sherpas are an ethnic group of devout Buddhists living in northeastern Nepal. They go everywhere on foot, carrying their property on their backs. But if walking is the Sherpas' fate, it has also been their fortune. The first ascent of Mount Everest, 60 years ago, sparked a tourism boom that draws thousands of visitors each year to hike amid the planet's tallest peaks. Sherpas serve as high-altitude porters for wealthy mountaineers; they also guide the larger number of trekkers who explore the altitudes under 18,000 feet. Sherpas own most of the 300-plus lodges and hotels and many of the companies that organize the treks.

My friend Nima Nuru Sherpa is one of thousands of Sherpa success stories. His family grew potatoes like everybody else, but by the time he was a teenager in the late 1960s, getting into the mountaineering business was every Sherpa boy's dream. "I was a porter," Nima says. "I carried 45 pounds all the way to Camp II on Everest. That's 22,000 feet, without oxygen!" Tireless, bright, and quick to pick up languages, Nima became a trekking guide. He saved his earnings and rented a house about 200 yards from the airstrip at Lukla. In 1993 he turned his house into Everest Lodge, which is now a successful hotel and restaurant business.

Most of the 70,000 or so Sherpas in Nepal aren't involved in the climbing or trekking industries. It's mainly in the Khumbu region that tourism transformed Sherpas' lives in a generation. The **influx** of Westerners has brought some of the comforts of modern life to the larger villages. In the town of Namche Bazaar, there are pool halls and pizza parlors, CD shops, and video rental counters. Tourism has made the Sherpas of Khumbu considerably richer than most of their neighbors. In Nepal as a whole, where 80 percent of the population are **subsistence** farmers, annual income is about $1,400. Sherpas involved in tourism can average five times as much.

LIVING ON THE EDGE
Namche Bazaar perches on the edge of a mountain. Residents plant potatoes on terraces carved into the mountainside.

The Effects of Change

There are mixed feelings about some of the modern conveniences made possible by the Sherpas' success. I learned this when I made the trek to the monastery at Tengboche to visit its head lama, or spiritual leader. The monastery sits at 12,700 feet. In the morning, the pink glow of dawn glistens on the snowy peaks of eight surrounding mountains, including Everest (29,035 feet) and its close neighbor Lhotse (loht-ZAY) (27,890 feet).

The lama, 68, is considered to be the **reincarnation** of the monastery's first lama. He has the title *rimpoche*, literally "precious one." When I ask the lama specific questions about Buddhist beliefs, he refers me to the monastery's website! And yet the rimpoche expresses considerable concern about the changes brought by modern ways to Sherpa traditions.

"When the Sherpas were farmers, with **yak** and cow, our life was good," he explains to me. "Now most people are in the trekking business, and that business goes down or up based on outside events.

"In the past we had no telephones here," the lama continues. "And it was no problem to be without a telephone. But now we have had telephones. We came to need them. Is this better?"

HEAVY TRAFFIC
In Namche Bazaar, yaks are herded past a downtown cybercafé.

Yes, say most Sherpas I spoke with. The Sherpa people, they will remind you, have always used outside influences to their own advantage. "The fact that we were separated from the rest of Nepal, way up in our high country, made it easy for the Sherpas to preserve our culture," says Ang Rita Sherpa. He heads the Himalayan Trust, in Kathmandu, Nepal's capital. Over a steaming bowl of spicy potato stew, Ang Rita fills me in. He points out that, despite their remote geographic setting, the Sherpas kept open minds about ideas from the outside.

The first British mountaineering expeditions made their way to Mount Everest in the early 20th century. They hired strong young Sherpas to be porters. The British expedition of 1953 was the first to reach the peak. The summit party consisted of one New Zealand climber, Edmund Hillary, and one Sherpa, Tenzing Norgay (whom you've met in the preceding article).

The conquest of majestic Mount Everest caught the imagination of the world. This brought many climbers to Khumbu each spring and fall.

City and Countryside

Despite events that sometimes interfere, Sherpas are optimistic about the future of the tourism industry. When it comes to predicting what will happen as more and more Sherpas leave Khumbu, there is less optimism. Educational opportunities are considered better in the large cities. Thousands now live in Kathmandu.

I saw the effects of so many Sherpas moving away when I visited the quiet village of Thamo. On a chilly, misty day in mid-September, I meet Pasang Namgyal Sherpa, a tiny figure with a latte brown face and wispy white hair. Pasang, 74, introduces me to his wife, Da Lhamu, 73. The couple invite me in for Sherpa tea.

Pasang and Da Lhamu have about 12 teeth left between them, but their smiles gleam as they tell me their life stories. "Well, if you're getting old," I ask afterwards, "who's going to take over this farm?" With that the cheery smiles disappear. The couple's son, it turns out, had taken a job on a climbing team and died in an avalanche in 2001. Pasang and Da Lhamu's only surviving child is their daughter, Phuti, who lives in Kathmandu.

In the city, 32-year-old Phuti and her family live in a four-room apartment. When I visit there, she and her husband, Nuru Nawang, a Sherpa from Solu, show me their place. They have a television set, a refrigerator and stove, a telephone, an indoor toilet, and tile floors. Nuru, who studied to be a Buddhist monk, says he would like to devote the days of the new and full moon to scripture readings, but his job as a trekking guide often makes that impossible.

Phuti introduces me to her daughter, Dawa, 6, and her son, Paldep, 5. They are in the elementary school there, studying both in English and Nepali. "The schools at home are no good," Phuti says decisively.

Not everything about the decision to live in Kathmandu is desirable, Nuru concedes. "Our children do not know the Sherpa language, or very little, anyway. When we take them to Khumbu, they don't know the names of the mountains. We want to pass on our beautiful culture and traditions," Nuru says. "But it is not so easy here."

The couple tell me that they definitely intend to go back to the Sherpa homeland—but not for many years to come.

It's this scattering of young people, rather than the modern influence of tourists themselves, that worries many Sherpas. After all, back in Khumbu, the old ways still persist. With rocks and branches, Sherpa farmers construct diversion channels beside the mountain streams to drive the waterwheels that grind their grain into flour.

READY FOR SCHOOL
Income from tourism allows some Sherpa parents to send their children to boarding schools such as this one in Kathmandu.

The same streams are used to spin the prayer wheels that dot Sherpa country. "In Khumbu, our traditions are maintained," Ang Rita Sherpa says.

THINK ABOUT IT! |||||||||||||||||||||||||||||||||

1 **Analyze Cause and Effect** Why are Sherpas particularly suited to success in the business of guiding mountain climbers and trekkers?

2 **Compare and Contrast** How has the development of mountain tourism changed life for many of the Sherpa people?

3 **Evaluate** How do the personal stories of Sherpa people contribute to the article?

BACKGROUND & VOCABULARY

influx *n.* (IHN-fluhks) a flowing in from elsewhere

reincarnation *n.* (ree-ihn-kahr-NAY-shuhn) in Buddhism, the belief in the rebirth of the soul in another physical body

subsistence *adj.* (suhb-SIHS-tuhns) getting by on the minimal resources necessary to support life

trekker *n.* (TREHK-ur) a person making a long, slow journey on foot; a recreational hiker

yak *n.* (YAK) a long-haired ox that is domesticated and used for work or raised for meat and milk

Death Zone

The atmospheric pressure at the top of Mount Everest is only 30 percent of what it is at sea level. With every breath, a climber who comes from low altitudes takes in less than a third as much oxygen as normal. That is why climbers must acclimatize, or get accustomed, to altitude before trying for a summit—and why above 26,000 feet the body begins a final breakdown.

Heart pounds, even at rest.

Hallucinations may occur.

Sample heart rate:
123 resting, 140 exercising

Civilization Stops

Humans can only adjust to this altitude very briefly. Therefore, there are no permanent settlements above this point anywhere on Earth.

Lungs expel more carbon dioxide; this disrupts the blood's chemical balance.

Kidneys discharge more water to correct the blood's acidity; this causes dehydration.

Sample heart rate:
85 resting, 140 exercising

The Death Zone

Climbers who challenge the Himalaya's highest peaks face dangers not just from falls and other accidents. At extreme altitudes, a climber's own body can become the enemy. At 8,000 feet—before they are even halfway up Mount Everest—climbers may develop acute mountain sickness. Symptoms include headache, fatigue, nausea, dizziness, vomiting, and more. When some climbers push past 8,000 feet, the sickness develops into conditions that could be fatal if they are not brought down off the mountain immediately.

Edema, the build-up of excess fluid in the body, is one such condition. For climbers at extreme altitude, edema frequently occurs in the brain or lungs. There it is a lethal threat. Ken Kamler is a doctor who has attempted the peak of Mount Everest four times. He says, "I've never gone to Everest without seeing someone suffer from cerebral or pulmonary edema." Cerebral edema takes place in the brain; pulmonary edema happens in the lungs.

In cerebral edema, plasma, one of the components of blood, leaks through the walls of small blood vessels in the skull. This leakage drives up pressure inside the skull. Scientists don't yet fully understand the reasons these blood vessels leak. It could be separation of normally tight junctions between cells lining the blood vessels. It could be swelling of the vessels themselves. Or it could even be a chemical that stimulates such growth in low-oxygen conditions, such as those found on Everest.

Pulmonary edema takes place in the lungs and is caused by squeezing of blood vessels. This squeezing creates high pressure in delicate blood vessels within the lungs, and they leak fluid that can cause the sufferer to drown on dry land. Once an afflicted climber has been brought down from the mountain, pulmonary edema is sometimes treated with nitric oxide, a chemical that dilates blood vessels and that the body produces normally. It's possible that a person's body may be especially prone to pulmonary edema if it hasn't been producing enough nitric oxide in the first place.

75% at 9,000 feet

Gulping Air

At this altitude nearly everyone feels the impact of the thin air.

Breathing speeds up and deepens as the body senses less oxygen in the blood.

Brain swells slightly, causing headache and nausea.

Kidneys increase the hormone that triggers production of more red blood cells.

Sample heart rate:
70 resting, 155 exercising

100% at Sea Level

Breathing Easy

At sea level, breathing is effortless.

Blood carries oxygen at almost full capacity.

Heart rate enjoys its greatest range.

Sample heart rate:
64 resting, 170 exercising

Under Pressure >

The scale to the right shows atmospheric pressure at different elevations on Mount Everest. Atmospheric pressure is the measure of how much pressure the air exerts on a surface, such as a human body. As the altitude rises, the atmospheric pressure goes down. Human lungs are best adapted for breathing in the atmospheric pressures found at lower altitudes. At high altitudes, breathing becomes a struggle. The percentages indicate the level of atmospheric pressure compared to the pressure at sea level.

EXPLORER'S JOURNAL

with Jimmy Chin

TRAINING AT YOSEMITE
Jimmy Chin honed his climbing skills at
Yosemite National Park in California
before moving on to the Himalaya.
Left: Chin hangs midair off the giant
rock formation called Half Dome.
Right: Chin stands at one of Yosemite's
highest points.

Few photographers will attempt the K7, a daunting mountain in Pakistan. Few will ski from the summit of Mount Everest just to frame a shot. Who do you call with such an assignment?

Feats of Climbing and Photography

National Geographic Explorer Jimmy Chin is a professional climber and skier. He is also one of the most sought-after expedition photographers. His passion for exploration, photography, and filmmaking has taken him on breakthrough expeditions around the planet. He has worked with the best adventurers, climbers, and skiers in the world. He's accompanied them on their most challenging expeditions, climbs, and ski descents. Chin is known for documenting their epic stories no matter what it takes. At times, this has meant enduring death-defying situations next to some of the best athletes in the industry.

Jimmy Chin's projects include many feats, all of them challenging. In China, he trekked across 300 miles of the Chang Tang Plateau, at 17,000 feet, filming this largely unexplored area for National Geographic. In Mali, West Africa, he documented the first ascents of the tallest freestanding sandstone towers in the world. In the Himalaya, he put up new climbing routes on some highly **technical** ascents.

In 2003, Chin accompanied Stephen Koch to the north face of Everest on his quest to snowboard the Seven Summits, the peaks of the highest mountains on each of the seven continents. Chin hit Everest again in 2004, climbing to the summit with famous mountaineers Ed Viesturs and David Breashears. He was shooting production stills and video for Universal Films. Viesturs called upon Chin again to accompany and photograph him on his final and successful expedition on Annapurna, in the Himalaya. This was Viesturs's last summit in his quest to climb the world's tallest peaks.

A few years later in 2006, Chin climbed and skied from the summit of Everest while shooting Kit DesLauriers's historic ski descent of the mountain. In the fall of 2011, after several attempts, Chin and his team made the first successful ascent of the Shark's Fin on Mount Meru—one of the most coveted and attempted climbs in the Himalaya.

Beginnings and Inspirations

"I was 12 when I had my first **epiphany** about the mountains. I went on a family vacation to Glacier National Park. The beauty of the West and the mountains of Glacier National Park really blew my mind. I was changed forever," remarks Chin. "I always knew I would return, and I did. I spent two summers working in Glacier . . . running up as many peaks as possible. I had also started rock climbing in Joshua Tree [National

dramatic actions distinguish Chin's photography. In addition, his work is known for his strong sense of **composition**. It is a rare gift to be able to pick up a camera for the first time and shoot a publishable photo.

But Chin was not new to composing within a frame. Chin's Chinese-American parents instilled the family's culture in their son by speaking Chinese at home and teaching him to draw Chinese characters using a brush and ink. He recalls: "I developed a talent for drawing the characters. I enjoyed drawing, but I loved the discipline of drawing characters. They demanded attention to detail, and an eye for balancing the different symbols inside the frame. The symbol for water, for example, has to be done perfectly or it will appear out of balance." Chin had many years of studying and drawing Chinese characters. He credits these for his ease with photo composition. "When I started shooting photos I didn't really think too much about composition; it came naturally."

Participatory Photographer

Something else that came to Chin naturally is his exceptional climbing and skiing ability. He is at ease on rocks and snow in the high mountains. This comfort has allowed him to practice a distinctive style of photography. He is the ultimate practitioner of what has been called "participatory photography." On expeditions, he balances his role as a team member with the demands of shooting assignment photos.

Chin feels that one of the most important parts of his job on any expedition is first to be a reliable team member and climber. The photography comes second. "The success of the expedition and safety are the priorities. As a climber, you face a lot of challenges on these expeditions. As a photographer, one of the great challenges is trying to be creative under fairly stressful conditions. You try to be smart about what you are shooting by anticipating the key moments and being efficient with your creative energy as well as your physical energy."

Chin participates in and shoots three or four major expeditions a year. "No two expeditions are the same, so you can't preconceive how an expedition will unfold," he says.

Park]. Spending time in the mountains and rock climbing became my passions."

Photography came later. During a climbing trip to Yosemite National Park, where he was training for an upcoming expedition to Pakistan, Chin took a photograph of El Capitan, a dramatic vertical rock formation, with a friend's camera. His friend submitted some photos of the climb to an outdoor clothing company. The company bought a single image—the one that Chin had taken. Encouraged by the sale of his first photo, Chin bought his own camera and hasn't looked back. His photography has won many awards, and in just a few years he became recognized as one of the best extreme mountain photographers in the profession. Wild mountain locations and

A STEEP CLIMB
Chin captured this photo from above as his partners carefully hiked along the South East Ridge of Mount Everest in 2006.

DON'T LOOK DOWN
Chin photographed his 2006
Everest expedition team member
who crossed from one side to the
other using a ladder, some ropes,
and a lot of courage.

"It's about sharing stories that inspire people, highlight the infinite human spirit, and open people's eyes to a different world."

—**Jimmy Chin**

Storytelling Through Photos

For Jimmy Chin, the art of photography is also the art of storytelling. Chin describes his meticulous technique as he approaches an expedition. He explains, "Often, I will make a shot list before a trip and continually revise and add to it during the trip. These lists help remind me of potential conceptual photos that might capture such ideas as teamwork, overcoming challenges, discovery, adventure, and success." He elaborates, "Photographing an expedition is like building a film—it's storytelling. I always look for transitional moments such as arriving at base camp, establishing climbing camps, the big storm, and summit day."

A favorite photo moment came at the end of the expedition to the Chang Tang Plateau in China. Chin and his companions were looking for the birthing grounds of the endangered chiru antelope. These Asian antelopes are hunted by poachers for their luxurious wool, which is used in the fashion industry. Among the expedition members was Galen Rowell, a great photographer and Chin's mentor. As the team climbed a mountain, they had to chop a hole through a snow **cornice** just below the summit.

"I had just poked my head through the hole," says Chin. "I looked down the ridge and saw Galen climbing toward me. My feet were dangling in space but I had my arms, ice axe, and camera free. I should have climbed out of the hole for a more secure footing, but I knew the moment would be lost, so hanging on by one arm I squeezed out three shots."

Jimmy Chin is passionate about his career and about capturing extreme, rarely-seen locations in photos and on film. "It's about sharing stories that inspire people, highlight the infinite human spirit, and open people's eyes to a different world," he comments. He hopes that the images and films from his expeditions will help him reach a greater goal. "Creating films and photographs through situations that few others could experience is my life's inspiration."

THINK ABOUT IT! ||||||||||||||||||||||||||||||||

1 **Summarize** What qualities and skills make Jimmy Chin a photographer in demand for challenging expeditions?

2 **Pose and Answer Questions** If you had an opportunity to talk with Jimmy Chin, what would you like to ask him about his aims and plans for his work?

3 **Synthesize** The article says Chin is the ultimate practitioner of the style called "participatory photography." What does the article tell you about the meaning of this term?

BACKGROUND & VOCABULARY

composition *n.* (kawm-puh-ZIHSH-uhn) the arrangement of parts in an artistic product

epiphany *n.* (ih-PIHF-uh-nee) a sudden insight or understanding

cornice *n.* (KOR-nuhs) in mountain climbing, an overhanging ledge of snow or ice projecting from the side of a ridge or peak

technical *adj.* (TEHK-nih-kuhl) in climbing, requiring specialized skills, not achievable through strength alone

The Sky Caves of Nepal

Adapted from "The Sky Caves of Nepal," by Michael Finkel,
in *National Geographic*, October 2012

Cliffside caves in the former kingdom of Mustang are giving up their secrets.

Questions About a Skull

The human skull was perched atop a boulder in a remote northern area of Nepal. Pete Athans, leading a team of mountaineers and archaeologists exploring the area, stepped into his harness and tied himself to a rope. Then he scrambled up the 20-foot boulder, secured by another climber.

When he reached the skull, he pulled on blue latex gloves to prevent his own DNA from contaminating the find. Then he gradually removed the skull from the rubble. Athans was almost certainly the first person to hold this skull in 1,500 years. He placed it in a padded red bag and lowered it to three scientists waiting below. They were Mark Aldenderfer of the University of California, Merced; Jacqueline Eng of Western Michigan University; and Mohan Singh Lama of Nepal's Department of Archaeology.

Aldenderfer was especially excited by the presence of two molars. Teeth can provide insights into a person's diet and health and indicate the person's general place of birth. Eng, a bioarchaeologist, swiftly determined that the skull likely belonged to a young adult male. She noted three healed fractures on the brain case, the part of the skull that contains the brain, and one on the right jaw. "Signs of violence," she mused. "Or maybe he was kicked by a horse?"

The boulder that Athans had climbed was directly below a soaring cliff, tan rock streaked with bands of pink and white. Toward the top were several small caves, which had been painstakingly dug from the brittle stone by hand. Erosion had caused the partial collapse of the cliff face, dislodging the skull. The same question was on everyone's mind: If a skull had tumbled out, what remained up there?

A Historic Kingdom

Mustang is a former kingdom in north-central Nepal. It is a dusty, wind-scoured place, hidden among the Himalaya, deeply carved by the Kali Gandaki River. It holds an extraordinary number of human-built caves.

Some caves sit by themselves. Others occur in groups, sometimes stacked in vertical neighborhoods eight or nine stories high. Some were dug into the cliff face, others tunneled from above. The total number of caves in Mustang, conservatively estimated, is 10,000.

No one knows who dug the caves, or why, or even how people climbed into them.

Seven hundred years ago, Mustang was a bustling place, a center of Buddhist scholarship and art, and most likely the trading connection between the salt deposits of Tibet and the cities of the Indian subcontinent.

According to anthropologists, nearby kingdoms began dominating Mustang in the 17th century. An economic decline set in, as cheaper salt became available from India. The great statues and brilliantly painted **mandalas** in Mustang's temples started crumbling, and soon the region was all but forgotten.

The Caves of Samdzong

In the mid-1990s, archaeologists from the University of Cologne and Nepal began peeking into some of the more accessible caves. They found several dozen bodies, all at least 2,000 years old. The bodies were aligned on wooden beds and decorated with copper jewelry and glass beads. These products were not locally manufactured, which confirmed that Mustang had been a trade route between other regions.

Pete Athans first glimpsed the caves of Mustang while trekking in 1981. Many of the caves appear impossible to reach, but Athans was an accomplished mountain climber, and he was stirred by the challenge they presented. It wasn't until 2007, however, that he obtained the necessary permits from the Nepalese government to try for the caves. Mustang immediately became, he says, "the greatest expedition of my life." This trip in the spring of 2011 was his eighth to the area.

During previous visits, Athans and his team had made some sensational finds in the caves, including beautiful murals and manuscripts. But they most wanted to find a cave with items from before the era of written records. Such a cave would shed light on the deepest mysteries: Who first lived in the caves? Where did these people come from? What did they believe?

The most promising site was a cave complex near a tiny village called Samdzong, just south of the Chinese border. Athans and Aldenderfer had visited Samdzong the year before and found a system of **funerary** caves there. On the first workday at the site in the spring of 2011, the team's photographer, Cory Richards, discovered the skull. The next morning, the climbers prepared to investigate the caves above.

Nearby was the local lama, or holy man, 72-year-old Tsewang Tashi. He would perform a Buddhist protection ceremony to remove troublesome spirits that could endanger the team's work. Sitting cross-legged in his maroon robe, he lit a small fire and filled a special cup with holy water from an old plastic Pepsi bottle. Then he chanted softly while ringing a brass bell and dipping his fingers in the water.

Athans, **rappelling** from the top of the cliff, maneuvered nimbly into the smallest cave. It was only five feet high and roughly six feet wide and six feet deep. This cave, it was clear, was once a hidden shaft tomb. When it was dug, only the very top of the shaft was visible. Bodies were lowered down the narrow shaft, and the hole was filled with rock. When the cliff face later collapsed, the entire cave was exposed, creating a cross-sectional view. **Carbon dating** later proved it had been about 15 centuries since the cave was sealed.

Aldenderfer divides cave use in Mustang into three general periods. First, as long as 3,000 years ago, the caves were burial chambers. (See the illustration at right.) Then, around 1,000 years ago, they became primarily living quarters. Finally, by the 1400s, most people had moved out of the caves and into traditional villages. The caves were still used—as meditation chambers, military lookouts, or storage units.

Most likely people first moved into the caves for protection. The Kali Gandaki Valley

Inside Tomb 5

Many of the caves in Mustang are empty, but one cave complex near Samdzong served as an ancient burial site. Archaeologists reconstructed the tomb and its contents.

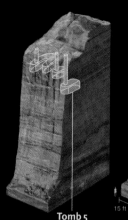

Collapsed area

15 ft

Tomb 5

A Quiet Resting Place

The adult found in Tomb 5 wore a gold-and-silver funerary mask. He was probably a local leader about 1,300 to 1,800 years ago. Artifacts found with his remains, such as iron daggers, a copper pot, and sacrificed animals reflect his status, as does a painting depicting a man, horses, and trees on his well-preserved wooden coffin.

Cliff Caves Exposed

Tunneled from the slope above, the tomb complex was situated away from the bustle of life in Mustang. To access some mortuary caves, narrow shafts led down to chambers. When the cliff face collapsed, it exposed the tombs, including Tomb 5 (reconstructed above).

Bronze mirror

Painted coffin front

A copper vessel may have once held chang, a barley beer.

Multicolored glass beads

Painted burial mask

Iron daggers

Iron tripod

Wood and bamboo cups

Tsampa, ground barley flour

Little is known about a child also found in the tomb.

Yak horns

The Mystery of the Bones

Human bones in this and nearby mortuary caves bear numerous cut marks—evidence, scientists say, that skin and muscle were removed before burial. It's possible this practice was a precursor to Tibetan Buddhism's "sky burial" tradition, in which bodies are left for vultures.

Horse and goat sacrifices

OLD AND NEW
Salt traders likely lived in the Nyphu caves in Mustang about 2,500 years ago. Today the site is a Buddhist monastery.

connected Asia's highlands and lowlands. It may have been frequently battled over. "People were scared," Aldenderfer says. Families, placing safety over convenience, moved into the caves. Some caves remained homes, and even today a few families live in them. "It's warmer in winter," says Yandu Bista, who was born in 1959 in a Mustang cave and lived in one until 2011. "But water is difficult to haul up."

The Treasures of Tomb 5

The cave Athans was exploring (shown on the preceding page), later named Tomb 5, was the size of a closet. The first thing he found was high-quality wood, cut into various planks and slats and pegs. Aldenderfer and Singh Lama eventually fitted the pieces together, making a box about three feet tall: a coffin.

Painted on the box was an image of a person riding a horse. "Probably his favorite horse," Aldenderfer guessed. Later the explorers found a horse skull in the cave.

On the 2010 trip to Samdzong, the team had found human remains in the two biggest caves on the cliff wall. There were 27 individuals, including men, women, and one child. Bedlike or **rudimentary** coffins appeared in those caves as well; however, they were made of much inferior wood, their construction was simpler, and they had no paintings.

> *"The people of Mustang should have pride in their own rich history."*
>
> **—Pete Athans**

Aldenderfer theorized that Tomb 5 was the burial plot of a high-ranking person, perhaps a local leader. Before leaving the cave, the ancient burial crew had made sure the corpse was royally adorned for the great beyond.

Athans scooped up a trove of beads from Tomb 5 and placed them in plastic sample bags. The garment they'd been sewn on was long disintegrated. There were more than 1,000 beads, made of glass in a half dozen hues. As lab studies later showed, the beads were of various origins, including the regions that are now Pakistan, India, and Iran.

Three iron daggers also emerged; they had gracefully curved hilts and heavy blades. Then a bamboo teacup with a delicate circular handle was found. A copper bangle. A small bronze mirror. A copper cooking pot and a ladle and a three-legged iron pot stand. Bits of fabric. An enormous copper cauldron, roomy enough to boil a beach ball.

Finally Athans sent down a funerary mask made of gold and silver pounded together, with facial features in high relief. The mask was probably sewn to fabric and draped over the face.

Nearly all the items in the cave had been imported from elsewhere. Today the area has so few resources that just gathering firewood requires hours of effort. How could a person from this place have gathered such riches? Salt, most likely. Controlling a piece of the salt trade may have been the equivalent of owning an oil pipeline today.

The entire haul left Aldenderfer struggling to place the find in historical context. "This is unique," he said. "Spectacular. This is rewriting the region's prehistory in a serious way."

The team left everything they found in the care of Samdzong's village leaders. The scientists removed only tiny sample chips and bits of bone to be studied in various labs. Athans also donated personal funds to endow a modest museum. "The people of Mustang should have pride in their own rich history," he says.

With so many exposed caves and an unknown number of hidden crypts [tombs], far more remarkable finds may be awaiting discovery. "It could be in the next cave we visit," says Aldenderfer. "It could be in a hundred more caves." As ever in Mustang, the cliffs hold secrets yet to be uncovered.

THINK ABOUT IT! ||||||||||||||||||||||||||||||

1 **Describe Geographic Information** How does the geographic information in the article help you understand Mustang's past and present?

2 **Form and Support Opinions** How do scientists respect the rights and desires of the people in the region? Do you think these efforts are adequate and appropriate?

BACKGROUND & VOCABULARY

carbon dating *n.* a method of determining the approximate age of a very old object using the amount of carbon 14 remaining in the material

funerary *adj.* (FYOO-nuh-ray-ree) having to do with burial and funeral practices

mandala *n.* (MUHN-duh-luh) a colorful geometric design used in Buddhist meditation and ritual

rappel *v.* (ruh-PEHL) to descend from a height by using a rope that is secured by another person or device

rudimentary *adj.* (roo-duh-MEHN-tuh-ree) elementary, basic, not fully developed

The Elusive
Snow Leopard

BY DOUGLAS H. CHADWICK

Adapted from "Out of the Shadows," by Douglas H. Chadwick,
in *National Geographic*, June 2008

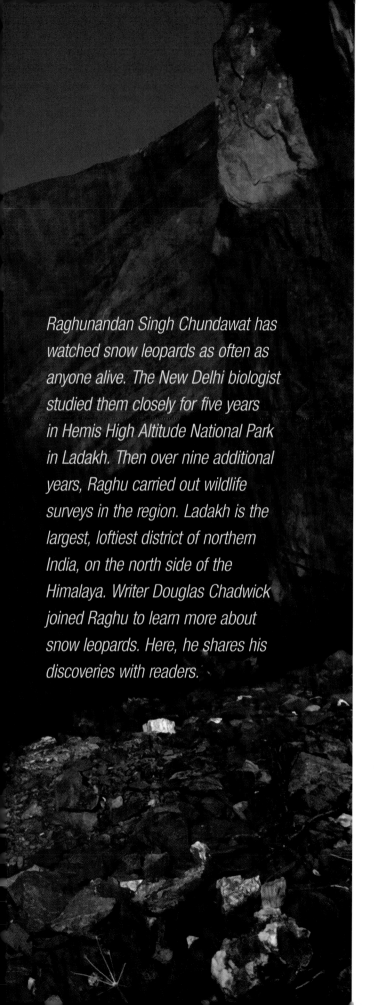

Raghunandan Singh Chundawat has watched snow leopards as often as anyone alive. The New Delhi biologist studied them closely for five years in Hemis High Altitude National Park in Ladakh. Then over nine additional years, Raghu carried out wildlife surveys in the region. Ladakh is the largest, loftiest district of northern India, on the north side of the Himalaya. Writer Douglas Chadwick joined Raghu to learn more about snow leopards. Here, he shares his discoveries with readers.

Looking for Leopards

When a snow leopard stalks prey among the mountains, it moves on broad paws with extra fur between the toes. It moves softly, slowly, "like the snow slipping off a ledge as it melts," Rahgu says. "If it knocks a stone loose, it will reach out a foot to stop it from falling and making noise." One might be moving right now. It would be perfectly silent, maybe close by. But where? That's always the question. That, and how many are left to see?

Raghu and I are setting up camp in Hemis, at about 12,000 feet. It's June, and the blue sheep have new lambs. We keep one eye on a group of sheep crossing a **scree** slope; we keep the other eye on the cliffs at its top. Leopards are ambush hunters—they like to attack from above. The common leopard of Asia and Africa relies on branches and leaves for concealment. The snow leopard loses itself among steep jumbles of stone. This is exactly the kind of setting one would favor. But I'm not holding my breath. Raghu has sighted only a few dozen in his whole career.

I imagine a leopard easing down the darkened slopes. It flows low to the ground. It has huge gold eyes and a coat the color of dappled moonlight on frost. Its body stretches four feet from nose to rump. Its tail is the most striking in the cat family. The tail is thick, mobile, and almost as long as the cat's body. The snow leopard sometimes uses its tail to send signals during social encounters. It may wrap its tail partway around itself like a scarf when bedded down in bitter weather. But the main function of this plume is to add balance. This is important in an environment with 1,000-foot drops.

Snow leopards are secretive, blend in well with their surroundings, and are usually solitary. They are most active at night and in the twilight hours of dusk and dawn. You'll never hear a snow leopard give away its location by roaring; it lacks the throat structure to roar.

NIGHTTIME PREDATOR
An endangered snow leopard prowls its mountainous territory by night.

Monitoring the Leopard Population

The snow leopard ranges across about a million square miles. Its range includes parts of 12 nations and imposing mountain ranges. Bound to high, cold, steep terrain, snow leopards have always remained at fairly low densities. However, they have become still more sparse during the past century.

Thousands were turned into pelts for the fashion trade. Since 1975, snow leopards have been officially protected under the Convention on International Trade in Endangered Species. However, they are still killed for their coats and other parts, worth a fortune on the illegal market. When snow leopards attack livestock, they may be killed by herders.

The current snow leopard population is estimated at only 4,000 to 7,000. The number may be less than half of what it was a century ago. Some authorities fear that the actual number may already have slipped below 3,500. Five of the countries in snow leopard range may have 200 or fewer. However, **grassroots** conservation efforts in a few areas are slowing the snow leopard's downward spiral.

Scientific information about the leopard is scarce. Raghu is the regional director of science and conservation for the nonprofit Snow Leopard Trust. He knows as much as anyone.

"A lot of research on snow leopard movements really tells you more about the limits of human abilities," he says. "You can only climb so many slopes before you grow exhausted or encounter sheer cliffs. It is just not possible to keep up." So Raghu tried capturing the cats to attach radios to them. He finally collared a female. But, like previous investigators, he was seldom able to monitor a signal for long. The animal dropped behind some ridge that blocked the transmission.

Over the years, biologists reported snow leopards covering territories of 5 to 14 square miles. American biologist Tom McCarthy first placed a satellite collar on one in Mongolia in

A CAT'S TERRITORY
A snow leopard marks its trail by rubbing its scent on a rock.

1996. He found it roaming a 386-square-mile area. "My guess is that the more satellite collars we get out, the larger we'll discover snow leopard territories to actually be," said McCarthy, who also works for the Snow Leopard Trust. Ten years passed before McCarthy placed the next satellite tag, this time in Pakistan. By mid-2007 the cat wearing it had revealed its movements over a range of some 115 square miles.

You can neither understand nor save a predator without doing the same for its prey. The snow leopard is the top carnivore of the **alpine** and subalpine **zones**. It strongly influences the numbers and whereabouts of hoofed herds over time. The hoofed animals, in turn, affect plant communities and other smaller organisms down the food chain. The leopards' presence, or absence, also affects the animals who compete with them for prey—wild dogs, jackals, foxes, bears, lynx, and others. These many interactions make snow leopards a governing force in the ecosystem—what scientists call a keystone species.

The snow leopard's range overlaps with the ranges of many other creatures. Therefore, protecting its habitat preserves homes for most of the mountain plants and animals.

Living with Leopards

Do snow leopards attack humans, as bears sometimes do? No, never, Raghu says. He once watched a village girl pulling on one end of a dead goat. She was unaware that the other end, hidden by a bush, was snagged in a snow leopard's jaws. She came away from the encounter unscratched. But a single leopard attack on a herd of livestock can plunge a family into desperate poverty.

Farming is marginal at best in Central Asia's cold, dry landscapes; traditional cultures depend mainly upon livestock to get by. Some herders operate from small villages on the mountainside. Others are nomadic, migrating long distances between seasonal pastures. Either way, they will inevitably have conflicts with snow leopards. The leopards are wired to select the unwary and the stragglers among wild hoofed animals. Villagers' herds are also hoofed animals. The cats can hardly help picking off a few domesticated

versions of their usual prey. At night, flocks are stuffed into low stone corrals by their human herders. A leopard can all too easily hop in to join them.

I was on a trek with conservationist Jigmet Dadul through the Sham area of the Ladakh Range. We made our way over the passes to the village of Ang. There we looked up Sonam Namgil. Three nights before, a snow leopard had leaped into the building where Namgil sheltered his herd. When Namgil opened the door in the morning, he found wide golden eyes staring back amid the bodies of nine goat kids and a sheep.

The herder reported: "Snow leopards have killed one or two animals in the pastures many times. This was the first problem at my home. Everybody wanted to finish this leopard."

Where losses mount, it's often because human hunting has made natural prey scarce. Overgrazing by livestock also reduces the natural capacity of rangelands to support native herds. Hungry leopards turn to the tame flocks for food. Then angry herders kill the cats in **retaliation**. Government enforcement of wildlife regulations in remote areas is weak. This means that a protection strategy has little chance of breaking these cycles unless it gains local support.

Saving the Snow Leopard

Religious leaders have recently spoken up on the leopards' behalf. Tsering Tundup is a Buddhist monk at the Rangdum monastery between the Zanskar Range and the main Himalaya. Speaking in the mountain-rimmed courtyard of the monastery, he said, "Whenever we have an opportunity, we talk to people and encourage them not to kill any being." Several people told me that the villagers listened when a lama farther up the valley condemned a series of revenge shootings of snow leopards.

The Dalai Lama, leader of Tibetan Buddhism, is widely followed in Central Asia. He has specifically urged followers to safeguard snow leopards; they should avoid wearing their pelts as part of traditional festive clothing. "People depend upon animals, but we must not use them for our luxury," he told me during an interview. "Wild animals are the ornaments of our planet and have every right to exist peacefully."

BALANCING ACT
This snow leopard's tail is on clear display. The leopard's tail helps it stay warm when the winter winds blow and keep its balance on steep mountain trails.

Financial incentives can also make a difference. Jigmet Dadul's employer, Snow Leopard Conservancy–India, helped set up Himalayan Homestays. This program steers tourists to the houses of herders who agree to protect snow leopards and their wild neighbors. Hosts have guests once every couple of weeks through the tourist season. This provides them with more than enough income to replace livestock lost to predators. Visitors pay about ten dollars a night and don't have to carry food or a tent. They receive a clean room and bed, meals with the family, and a warm introduction to the culture of the region.

The conservancy donates funds to cover livestock pens with stout wire mesh. Rodney Jackson is the pioneering snow leopard researcher who founded the conservancy. He says, "We

figure each project to predator-proof the corrals of a village this way saves an average of five leopards." The organization launches small-scale livestock insurance programs as well. In the case of the marauding cat that was stuck inside the farm building in Ang, the ending was good. The news reached the ears of a local Homestays nature guide. By insisting that they let authorities relocate the animal, the young man saved the snow leopard from being beaten to death.

Snow leopard numbers for Hemis National Park and other strongholds in Ladakh look stable or even on an upward trend. Blue sheep and urial sheep, which snow leopards prey on, are also making a comeback. Regional wildlife departments, nonprofit groups, and the mountain villages can all claim the credit for this success together.

Other Challenges

Success stories like these are rare in other parts of snow leopard range. The cats continue to vanish from many locales like snow patches under a summer sun. Sprawling China is home to the the largest number of snow leopards—perhaps 2,000. Most are spread across the wrinkled immensity of Tibet. Yet authorities worry that the cats are being heavily hunted in China, the world's largest market for illegal tiger and leopard products. The second-largest population of the predators may now belong to Mongolia, which probably holds 800 to 1,700.

Mongolia is a nation of herders. Livestock outnumber the 2.6 million humans 15 to 1. An admirable network of parks and reserves has been established in western Mongolia. Mantai Khavalkhan is the superintendent of four reserves

in Mongolia's Altay region. He explains that the **infrastructure** to manage the reserves is thin. "We don't have enough staff to protect their core wildlands from heavy livestock grazing, poaching, forest fires, and illegal woodcutting," Khavalkhan notes. Yet the leopard appears to be holding its own where conservation efforts have won local support.

The Turgen Range, part of the Altay Mountains in Mongolia, saw some heavy wildlife **poaching** in the past. It has become a stronghold for ibex (a type of antelope) and their predators now. One of the reasons is a grassroots antipoaching patrol known as the Snow Leopard Brigade.

Ganbold Bataar is its founder and current chief. Toward evening, three horsemen driving their flocks home galloped over to visit our camp. They all considered themselves volunteer members of the antipoaching brigade. They knew the local mother snow leopard well. She'd had three new cubs the previous year, they said. The two from her earlier litter had gone off to establish territories of their own on the mountain slopes just across the river. One had appeared prowling the iron-red ledges there just recently. One of the horsemen said simply, "I'm proud to live in a place with snow leopards."

A small, soft-spoken woman named Bayarjargal Agvaantseren has found another way to enlist local communities in conservation. Twice every year, this former schoolteacher sets out from the Mongolian capital, Ulaanbaatar (oo-lahn-BAH-tohr). She visits some of the 24 herder communities she has engaged in a handicrafts project called Snow Leopard Enterprises (SLE); it is a program of the Snow Leopard Trust.

Most herder families used to sell the soft underfur of goats—cashmere—to middlemen, earning about $600 a year. Thanks to Agvaantseren, women in the community now also make various products using wool from their goats, sheep, yaks, and camels. My favorites were doll mice with whiskers of stiff yak tail hair—toys for little cats, designed to save big ones.

An independent review in 2006 found no poaching of snow leopards in areas where SLE operates. Agvaantseren just added eight more communities and intends to expand a **microcredit** scheme that lets members borrow

BUILT FOR POWER
Long, muscular hind legs enable snow leopards to leap great distances.

money to buy items such as spinning wheels or material to improve corrals. "People hear good reports from neighbors, and they come to us now asking how to join," she said.

The Western model of establishing nature sanctuaries in landscapes unoccupied by humans simply doesn't fit much of Asia. Projects like the Homestays program in India and the handicrafts business in Mongolia seem to fit very well. Though they cover only a small fraction of the species' homeland so far, they make live leopards more valuable to more people each year. In doing so they mark a path toward the conservation of high mountain ecosystems.

THINK ABOUT IT! ||||||||||||||||||||||||||||

1 **Make Inferences** How would you describe the writer's feelings about the snow leopard?

2 **Analyze Cause and Effect** How does local support contribute to the success of snow leopard conservation efforts?

3 **Make Predictions** What will happen to the snow leopard populations in the areas mentioned in the article? Explain your answers.

Shafqat Hussain
National Geographic Explorer

Adapted from "Shafqat Hussain, Conservationist," nationalgeographic.com

National Geographic Explorer and conservationist Shafqat Hussain was born in Pakistan's lowlands, but he always felt drawn to the mystery and majesty of the region's highest mountains. In the remote Baltistan region, he learned, the economy depended on herding. Snow leopards killed village goats and sheep. In return, communities killed the cats. The cats became endangered.

Concern for the local economy and an extraordinary species in peril led Hussain to create Project Snow Leopard. This ingenious low-cost insurance program compensates local herders for each animal killed by a snow leopard. The effect is to stabilize the economy and to deter the killing of cats. The self-funding system requires herders to pay a small premium for each animal they own. Villages use surplus funds from the nonprofit program for civic projects. Five thousand people throughout ten villages participate in the ever-expanding project. Meanwhile, about 50 snow leopards benefit from the plan's protection. This is approximately one-fifth of the entire species left in Pakistan.

Although conservation of an endangered species lies at the heart of the program, meeting human needs is equally vital to its mission. "Conservation should not come at the expense of poor farmers," Hussain says. "Helping this incredible endangered species and the people who share its environment are equally important to us. Not one or the other, but both."

K2:
Danger on the Savage Mountain

Adapted from "K2: Danger and Desire on the Savage Mountain," by Chip Brown, *National Geographic*, April 2012

At 28,251 feet, K2 has a singular place in high-altitude mountaineering. Though 784 feet lower than Mount Everest, it is known as the mountaineer's mountain and a more difficult climb. As of 2010 Everest had been successfully climbed 5,104 times; K2, just 302. Roughly one K2 climber has died for every four who've succeeded. In the summer of 2011, a team of experienced climbers, including National Geographic Explorer Gerlinde Kaltenbrunner, set out to conquer the "savage mountain."

HIGH-ALTITUDE TRUDGE
International 2011 K2 North Pillar
Expedition members climb a snow slope
below Camp II.

STRUGGLE UP THE RIDGE

For most of July and half of August the six members of the International 2011 K2 North Pillar Expedition had been shuttling up and down the forbidding North Ridge of K2. Theirs was the only party on the remote Chinese side of K2, on the China-Pakistan border. The mountaineers were climbing the ridge (although "ridge" understates the steepness of the terrain) without bottled oxygen or high-altitude porters.

What the team lacked in numbers it made up for in experience. The two climbers from Kazakhstan—Maxut Zhumayev, 34, and Vassiliy Pivtsov, 36—were making their sixth and seventh attempts to summit K2. Dariusz Załuski, a 52-year-old Polish videographer, was a veteran of three attempts. Tommy Heinrich, a 49-year-old photographer from Argentina, had made two K2 expeditions but had also failed to summit.

Most notable was Gerlinde Kaltenbrunner, a 40-year-old former nurse from Austria who was on her fourth trip to K2. If she succeeded this time, she would become the first woman in history to climb without supplemental oxygen all

14 of the world's highest peaks. She was leading the expedition with her husband, Ralf Dujmovits, 49, who had already climbed all of the highest peaks (all but one without bottled oxygen) and is Germany's foremost high-altitude mountaineer.

It had taken 42 days for the six climbers to establish several camps connected by thousands of feet of rope. The route included everything from vertical rock and ice to **avalanche**-raked slopes of chest-deep snow. They had pushed themselves to break trail in heavy snow, haul gear, shovel out campsites, pitch tents, and melt ice. Many times they gave up their gains on the mountain, going down to sleep at the lower elevation of Advanced Base Camp.

On August 16 they set out on what would be their only real chance for the summit. The snow that had been falling for much of the summer had started again. They reached Camp I, at the foot of the ridge, that day. Avalanches roared and more than a foot of snow fell overnight. They waited there, hoping the snow on the slopes above would come down before they continued their ascent.

RISKY CROSSING
Even before the team started climbing, they encountered dangers. Here, a strong current in the Shaksgam River nearly swallows a camel carrying supplies to the team's base camp in China.

On August 18 at 5:10 A.M. they decided to push ahead to Camp II. Two avalanches had already swept over their route up a long **gully**. Around 6:30 A.M. Ralf stopped the team's advance. So dangerous were the snow conditions he could no longer ignore his gut feelings.

"Gerlinde, I am going back," he said.

The couple had made a pact that neither would stand in the other's way if one wanted to continue and the other did not. Having never been to the top of K2, Gerlinde was willing to take risks that Ralf, who had, was not. But now, despite their agreement, despite knowing the delay might cost her chance to reach the summit, Ralf begged his wife to come down with him. "Ralf was yelling that the route is very, very avalanche prone. He was shouting desperately," Maxut said later in a video on his website. "And Gerlinde shouted in return that now is the moment when the fate of the climb will be decided. If we turn around today, on the 18th, we are not making the period of good weather."

"I was really afraid I would never see her again," Ralf explained later.

Gerlinde watched as Ralf handed out his group gear to the rest of the team and descended into the mist. And then, in what may be the best example of her **tenacity** and will, she returned to the task at hand. "It's not that I was indifferent to the risk," she said afterward. "But my gut feeling was good."

As Ralf had feared, the snow on the slope began to rip loose, three small slides in succession. Tommy, climbing almost 200 feet below, was knocked upside down. Snow stuffed his nose and mouth. Only the fixed rope kept him from being flushed off the mountain. He was able to dig himself out, but the slide had refilled

the broken trail, and eventually he too turned back.

So now they were four: Gerlinde, Vassiliy, Maxut, and Dariusz. The job of breaking trail seemed endless. Sweep the snow aside, crack the crust with your knee, compact what's underneath, step up, slip back. Repeat and repeat and repeat. After 11 hours they rested at Shoulder Depot Camp, below Camp II, and spent a miserable night crammed into a two-person tent. The following day they negotiated the most difficult sections of the ridge and reached Camp II, at 21,654 feet, where they changed into warm down suits. On Saturday, August 20, they slogged on to Camp III, arriving in the afternoon exhausted and chilled to the bone.

ON THE EDGE
Relying on the front points of her crampons—spikes attached to her boots—Kaltenbrunner climbs the steep rock-and-snow pitches up to Camp II.

They drank coffee with honey and warmed their hands and feet over their gas stoves. All night the tent walls snapped and shuddered in the strong wind.

Better weather finally arrived on Sunday, August 21, lifting everyone's spirits and helping to carry the team to Camp IV. They were now at nearly 26,250 feet, in the so-called death zone where the body is unable to adjust to the oxygen-depleted air. Thinking becomes impaired, and the simplest tasks can take forever. They spent the afternoon sharpening their **crampons** and melting snow. Toward evening they stood outside their tents, pitched in a notch of rock above an appalling void that plunged nearly two miles to the glacier below. Two thousand feet above lay the glistening white summit of K2.

SCALING THE SUMMIT

August 22 was a morning that was like a gift. The gales were gone, the snow had quit, and the sky ran blue and cloudless all the way to the black edge of space.

Around 7 A.M., Gerlinde, Vassiliy, Maxut, and Dariusz set out from Camp IV for a crowning point of Earth. They were climbing up a steep chute of ice high on the mountain's north face. The way up was unfamiliar and difficult to see. With only a third of the oxygen at sea level, snow up to their chests in places, and stinging blasts of wind-driven snow, the group made painfully slow progress.

Gerlinde reached Ralf on the radio at Advanced Base Camp. Since turning back, he had devoted himself to supporting the summit party, passing on weather forecasts, advice, and encouragement. Though miles away, he could see that the best place to cross was below the lip of a long, thin **crevasse** that ran the width of the slope. There the snow tended to be not as deep, and the natural break in the slope would lessen the chance of the climbers triggering an avalanche. He helped guide them to the crevasse and watched as their figures, no bigger than commas on a page of paper, began edging across the ice. Above them were bulges of ice that protruded from the steep slope like dormers—windows that project vertically from a roof.

K2 North Pillar Expedition

This map shows the expedition's key camps and route to the summit. K2 is located in the Karakorum Mountains, a subrange of the Himalaya.

PAKISTAN

CHINA

K2 North Glacier

N

To Advanced Base Camp
Altitude 4,650 m

SUMMIT
8,611 meters (28,251 ft)
August 23, 2011

Japanese Couloir

△ Bivouac site
8,300 m
August 22
(Est. August 22)

CAMP IV
7,950 m
August 21
(Est. August 21) ⛰

Tent site
7,900 m

CAMP III
7,250 m
August 20
(Est. July 22) ⛰

Tent site
7,300 m

PAKISTAN

CHINA

CAMP II
6,600 m
August 19
(Est. July 14) ⛰

North Ridge

Northwest Ridge

Shoulder Depot Camp
6,250 m
August 18
(Est. July 7) ⛰⛰

⛰ Middle Camp
5,950 m

CAMP I
5,300 m
Summit push: August 16-17
(Established July 5)
⛰

ASIA
KAZ.
PAK. ☐ **K2**
NEPAL CHINA
INDIA
TAIWAN

43

The bulges might protect the climbers if avalanches swept down the mountain toward them.

Nearing the rocky left edge, they turned to move directly up the slope. They'd been climbing for 12 hours, and they were 984 feet below the summit. On the radio Ralf urged Gerlinde to return to Camp IV for the night now that they had broken the trail up to that point and knew the way.

"You cannot sleep there. You cannot relax," he told her.

"Ralf," said Gerlinde, "we are here. We don't want to go back."

With the sun low in the west, they stopped to prepare a site for a tiny tent. For an hour and 20 minutes they hacked at the ice until they had a level platform four feet wide, five feet long. They anchored the tent with two ice screws and a pair of ice axes. By 8:15 they were all inside, a stove hanging from the ceiling with a pot of melting snow. Gerlinde made some tomato soup. The temperature was minus 13 degrees. The plan was to rest until midnight, then resume the push for the prize.

THE LAST PUSH

At one in the morning Vassiliy, Maxut, and Gerlinde started up the steep grade by the light of their headlamps. Gerlinde swung her arms in big circles to warm up, but she couldn't feel her fingers, and she was having trouble unclipping from the rope. Maxut's feet felt like blocks of ice. They retreated to the tent to try to get warm. Gerlinde shivered uncontrollably.

They set out again around 7 A.M. as another clear morning dawned. It was now or never. Gerlinde carried spare batteries, extra mittens, toilet paper, a second pair of sunglasses, bandages, drops for snow blindness, and other medical supplies. Inside her suit she tucked the half-liter of water she had managed to melt. In her pack it would freeze.

They worked their way up the slope toward a ramp of snow that angled up to the summit ridge. They were still suffering from the cold but by 11 A.M. could see they would soon be in the sun. At 3 P.M. they reached the base of the ramp. They were exhilarated to discover that they sank only

> *"It's not that I was indifferent to the risk,"* she
> *said afterward. "But my gut feeling was good."*
>
> —**Gerlinde Kaltenbrunner**

to their shins in the snow. But soon the snow was chest deep. They had to switch the exhausting lead position every 10 steps. Gerlinde thought, it's not possible that we've come so far up and will have to turn back now.

Desperate for an easier way, they stopped climbing in single file at one point. Ralf was astonished to see their track split into three lines as they searched for better footing. Ahead lay a band of snow-patched rocks that proved easier to negotiate. Climbing single file again, Gerlinde changed places with Vassiliy and sank only up to her knees. With a surge of energy and hope she clambered out of the ramp and onto the ridge where the wind-packed snow was like a sidewalk. It was 4:35 P.M. She could see the summit dome.

She sipped from her water bottle. Her throat was cracked. It hurt to swallow. It was too cold to sweat, but they were all getting dehydrated just from panting for air. When Vassiliy caught up, he told Gerlinde to go on to the summit. He would wait for Maxut so they could climb to the top together. They exchanged a few words, and then she walked the final steps to the **apex** of K2.

It was 6:18 P.M. She wanted to share the moment with Ralf, but when she opened the radio she couldn't speak. There were mountains in every direction. Mountains she had climbed. Mountains that had stolen the lives of her friends and nearly claimed hers too. But never had she invested so much in a mountain as the one under her boots at last. With the world at her feet, she turned from one point of the compass to another.

"It was one of the most powerful experiences of my life," she said of that moment later. "I felt as if I were one with the universe. It was so strange on one hand to be extremely exhausted and on the other to be getting so much energy from the view."

Fifteen minutes later Maxut and Vassiliy arrived, shoulder to shoulder. Everyone embraced. Half an hour later Dariusz staggered up, his hands suffering from having taken his gloves off to change batteries on the video camera. It was 7 P.M. Their shadows reached far across the top of K2, as the shadow of the mountain itself reached for miles to the east, and a beautiful golden light began to shine on the world.

THINK ABOUT IT!

1 **Describe Geographic Information** Describe the geographic features of K2, using the visuals and the text as sources of information.

2 **Form and Support Opinions** After reading this article, would you want to climb K2 someday? Explain why or why not, citing details from the article to support your opinion.

BACKGROUND & VOCABULARY

apex *n.* (AY-pehks) the uppermost point or top

avalanche *n.* (AV-uh-lanch) a large mass of snow, ice, earth, or rock sliding down a mountainside or over a steep cliff

crampons *n.* (KRAM-pahnz) the spikes attached to shoes to make it easier to grip the surface

crevasse *n.* (kruh-VAS) a deep crack in a glacier

gully *n.* (GUH-lee) a deep, water-worn ravine or gorge

tenacity *n.* (tuh-NAS-uh-tee) the persistence or quality of sticking to a behavior or belief; toughness

Document-Based Question

The Himalayan region is geographically and culturally like no other place on Earth. The mountains include the highest peaks on the planet, and the people who live there have unique cultures that blend thousands of years of tradition with contemporary ways of life.

DOCUMENT 1 Primary Source

Picking up the Trash

For 60 years, climbers have dumped gear and trash on the way to the top of Mount Everest. Though tons of garbage are removed every year from the base camps, the Sherpas and others were concerned about the trash left on the climbing routes. In 2010, two Nepali groups launched expeditions to remove seven tons of waste from the higher routes on the mountain.

Nepali clean-up expedition on Mount Everest, 2010

CONSTRUCTED RESPONSE

1. Why do you think Nepali groups are concerned about trash being left on Mount Everest?

DOCUMENT 2 Primary Source

Blogging from Everest

In the spring of 2012, an elite climbing team headed by National Geographic Explorer Conrad Anker set out to summit Mount Everest. Fifty-five days after arriving at base camp, they made it to the top of Everest. National Geographic writer Mark Jenkins was on the climb and blogged the expedition. In this last entry of the blog, Jenkins reflects on why some are so drawn to this challenge.

> Climbing Everest is not curing cancer. It is a narcissistic [self-centered] pursuit, not a noble one. But, there is grandeur in the endeavor [act]. . . . Because Everest is so high and so indifferent, it calls upon every mountaineer, at some point during the climb, to rise to his or her better self—that person inside us all who has unquestioned courage, who will sacrifice without doubt, who will commit without complaint, who will put life on the line. This is the answer to the inevitable question: Why? Because: The highest mountain in the world, Mount Everest, expects of you, demands of you, to reach for the highest qualities inside yourself.

from Mark Jenkins, "Dispatch #58: Coda," ngm.nationalgeographic.com/everest, May 29, 2012

CONSTRUCTED RESPONSE

2. What generalizations might you make about the motivation of people who climb Mount Everest?

DOCUMENT 3 Secondary Source

Taming the Mountain

The success rate of climbers on Mount Everest has more than tripled since 1990, largely due to more guides and better gear. The number of attempts on the summit has also increased greatly since Edmund Hillary's successful climb in 1953.

CONSTRUCTED RESPONSE

3. What effects, both positive and negative, do you expect the the positive trend in successful climbs to have on the Everest region?

Climbing Mount Everest, 1953–2012

Look at the year 2000. The dark part of the bar represents the number of successful summits, 145, a 24 percent success rate. The light part of the bar represents the number of people who made it to Base Camp or above, about 345.

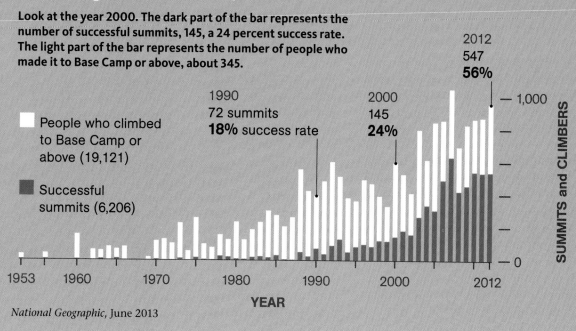

Legend:
- People who climbed to Base Camp or above (19,121)
- Successful summits (6,206)

1990
72 summits
18% success rate

2000
145
24%

2012
547
56%

National Geographic, June 2013

PUT IT TOGETHER

Review Think about your responses to the Constructed Response questions and what you have learned from this book about the people who live in and visit the Himalaya.

List Main Idea and Details Make a list of main ideas and details that describe people who have climbed Mount Everest, success rates of expeditions, and the impact of humans on the Everest environment.

Write How and why do people interact with Mount Everest? Use your notes to write a paragraph that answers this question.

INDEX

IIIIIIIIIIIIIIIIIIIIIIIIIIIIIIIIIIIIIIIIIIIIIII

SKILLS